poems
love and relationships

Love,
hAte
BeSt and my
MatE

In memory of my mother, Marcia Grail
– Polly Peters

To Caroline, Henrietta, Sarah and all the pupils at
St Peter's High School, Gloucester
– Andrew Fusek Peters

This collection copyright © Andrew Fusek Peters and Polly Peters 2004

Editor: Kay Barnham
Designer and illustrator: Jane Hawkins

Published in Great Britain in 2004
By Hodder Children's Books
This paperback edition published in 2005

A catalogue record of this book is available from the British Library

ISBN: 0340 893877

Printed and bound in Great Britain by Clays Ltd, St Ives plc

The paper used in this book is a natural recyclable product made from
wood grown in sustainable forests. The hard coverboard is recycled.

Hodder Children's Books
A division of Hodder Headline Limited
338 Euston Road, London NW1 3BH

Contents

Foreword 4

LOVE 5

HATE 62

MY BEST MATE 96

Index by title 122

Index by author 124

Acknowledgements 126

Biography 128

Foreword

In compiling this collection, we were looking for poetry from past and present that really hit the spot. What we found – ranging from Roman rhymes to email epics – fascinated us. The spitting hate expressed by an Anglo-Saxon poet and the summer romance dwelt on by the fourteenth-century Dafydd Ap Gwilym are as relevant today as when they were first written.

The three subjects – *love, hate* and *my best mate* – cover a huge spectrum of experiences and feelings. There are lyrical pieces alongside text-message sonnets and hauntingly sad poems juxtaposed with in-your-face humour. You'll also find the latest poetry by Brian Patten and Helen Dunmore, plus a wealth of new talent and old favourites.

We hope you enjoy reading this collection as much as we enjoyed putting it together.

Andrew Fusek Peters and Polly Peters

HIS FIRST LOVE

Falling in love was like falling down the stairs
Each stair had her name on it
And he went bouncing down each one like a
 tongue-tied lunatic
One day of loving her was an ordinary year
He transformed her into what he wanted
And the scent from her
Was the best scent in the world
Fourteen she was fourteen
Each day the telephone
Each day an email
Each day he'd text her
Each day was unfamiliar
Scary
And the fear of her going weighed on him
 like a stone

And when he could not see her two nights
It seemed a century had passed
And meeting her and staring at her face
He knew he would feel as he did for ever
Hopelessly in love
Sick with it
Not even knowing her second name yet
It was the first time
The best time
A time that would last for ever
Because it was new
Because he was ignorant it could ever end
It was endless

Brian Patten

BOY WITH GREEN HAIR

I saw him on the beach one morning, only
a boy, not much older than me, but his hair was
dyed green as grass on a wet summer's day.
I watched it lap against his neckline like
seaweed flotsam on a ragged shore,
his skin shock-white beneath it like
a plant grown under glass,
drained of sunlight
and prized
for it.

I saw him winging down the sand, as quick as
Mercury, but shod in shabby, broken, plastic trainers.
His eyes, as sharp as lasers, sliced the sunlight
into patterns which we glanced through at each
other, making plans and hatching formless
plots. And then, the tide surged up the sand,
ripping up our chances and springing us
apart. 'He's just a boy,' I told myself.
'And boys are stupid, any
way. Everybody
knows that.

I also know that I will see him again, one day
when I am brave enough to date green hair and he is
old enough to recognize a tidal surge about to hit.
And I will search the face of every passing
stranger for that skin as white as winter under
glass. And in a moment, waiting like a
silent wish, our eyes will meet again,
and I will ask, and he'll reply,
'Hey, haven't I seen
you somewhere
before?'

Pauline Fisk

MY MATE FANCIES YOU

Really fit, Really fit,
My mate thinks you're really it!

Chew her gum and wiggle her hips,
Take her out for fish 'n' chips.

Really it, Really it!
My mate thinks you're really fit!

Flash her eyes and foot in the door,
Admire those biceps, shout out 'Phwoarr!'

Really fit, Really fit,
My mate thinks you're really it!

Soon she'll have him under her thumb,
Get those hands around that bum!

Really it, Really it!
My mate thinks you're really fit!

Truth is out, I gotta admit,
It's not my mate who thinks you're fit...

Really fit, Really fit!
Guess which one the love bug's bit?

How I dream of being kissed,
Lips apart for the young-tongue-twist...

Really it! Really it!
I'm the one who thinks you're fit!

Polly Peters

ASNOGSTICK

Felt
Incredibly
Right
Scary
Though!

Seriously
Navigating
Over
Gums!

Steve Fisher

LOVE KEPT SECRET
– AN EXCERPT

We walked when trees were full of leaf,
My darling had my true belief,
Summoned sweet this kiss of ease,
Our life beneath the birch-bark trees.
Hidden in our woodland home
On distant shores, together roam
Together, singing in the wood,
Dug the seed that grew to good,
Wove the branches, made a nest
My girl and I, together best.
Who could ever see to blame
This wander down the leafy lane?
Together smiled the double face,
Lip to lip we laugh, embrace;
And lay together in the shade,
Friends forgotten that we made,
Drifting hours with drinking mead,
Together loving, living need –
Stay true with urgent secrecy:
Now you shall hear no more from me.

Dafydd ap Gwilym, 14th century Welsh,
A version by Andrew Fusek Peters

LOVE LETTERS

For my birthday,
Mark sent me an email
That burst open like a water lily
And showered our computer screen
With happy, hoppy frogs
(Until Dad deleted it).

For an Easter surprise,
James sent me a fax
That rattled and clattered
Out of our old machine
Leaving black chickens on limp paper
(Which somehow flapped into the bin).

For Christmas Day,
Leo left me a jolly, holly voicemail
That jangled once,
Then vanished on the icy air
(When Mum recorded over it).

For Valentine's Day,
Michael sent me a text greeting,
Which was extremely witty and clever,
And exactly the same as the one he sent
To Jane and Heather and Zita and...
(So we all sent him a rather rude message back.)

At break this morning,
For no special reason at all,
Joe passed me a crumpled, smudgy note
On a scrap of paper, still warm
From his shy hand.
I have read it one hundred and thirty-two times,
But it hasn't disappeared. Yet.

(I don't think it ever will.)

Clare Bevan

ASKING OUT

I'd love to ask her out.
But how to go about it
is the thing.

Do I say,
'Fancy the cinema on Saturday?'

What if she says,
'Yes I do but not with you!'

Do I reply,
'That's OK.
I heard it's a crap film anyway!'

Then what if it gets round
she turned me down?

It isn't worth the risk.

And it would be just as big
a mess if she says,
'Thanks. The answer's yes!'

What do I talk about?
I guess football and kick boxing's
out. What do you talk about
with girls?

Should I try to hold her hand?
What if my hands are sweaty,
or my armpits or my feet?

How do you snog?
What if I've got bad breath?
How can I tell?
Is breathing into your hand
any sort of test?

Things might be much simpler,
it seems to me, if we practised this
sort of stuff in PSHE.

Jim Hatfield

OVERHEARD BEHIND THE LOCKERS

Matt Simpson

FIRST KISS

A most momentous entry this;
My first, my very first real kiss!
We'd been out clubbing it in town;
Came out and found it pouring down.
She said, 'Come on, share my umbrella.
I wouldn't share with any fella.'
We had to huddle close together
And put our arms round one another.
Our faces touched; I didn't speak
But pressed my lips against her cheek —
Well, actually, against her nose
'Cos at that moment she just chose
To turn her head, which made me miss.
She laughed, 'That's not a proper kiss.
A proper kiss is done like this.'
We stood still in the pouring weather
Our lips just kind of clamped together
All warm and moist for quite some time:
It was superb, it was sublime.
We stopped for breath, then did some more:
I lost count after twenty-four.

My life has changed. The world is ace.
Got to close now – but watch this space.

WEDNESDAY, 1st MARCH

I couldn't wait today at school
to see her. She was very cool.
I said, 'Last night I was dumbstruck.'
She laughed and said, 'Beginner's luck!
You needed practice obviously.
See you around sometime – maybe.'
And off she went back to her room.
I am engulfed in hopeless gloom.

Eric Finney

BEAN PICKING

Bean picking one summer with Mike
and two girls I hardly knew.

It was back-breaking work
for little cash, but simple.
Even I couldn't make a hash of it.

And Mike was a smooth talker
who rolled from the cradle
bright side up.

He spent most of his time impressing
the girls, I envied his line
in patter, his quick delivery.

I liked to think I might learn
his technique.

And then when it rained, we played around
with the girls on the hay in the barn,
all innocent stuff really,
jumping off bales in daredevil stunts.

Till suddenly the playing stopped
and Mike and Brenda paired off,
while Sally was left with me.

I took her hand and we stumbled along
the rows of beans in the rain,
and somewhere in my chest,
in my big kid heart, I felt
the rumblings of first love.

Brian Moses

FONE FANTASY

They only eva use me
2 txt luv notes 2 1 anuva
dnt they reliz
I need 2 b stroked
Caressed
Prt of the actn?
fones have feelings 2

Alison Chisholm

IT'S OUT AT LAST

Love has come at last. The very idea
that I'd hide it makes me more ashamed
than openly confessing. Won over
by my muse's supplication, Cythera's Goddess
has brought me to him, placed him in my arms.
What Venus promised, she has fulfilled.
Let them tattle who have missed their chance.
I'll not entrust the news to a sealed letter
that none may read off it before my lover does.
I loathe to wear a mask in deference
to what the world may say. Let everyone hear
That we have come together – each of us
deserving the other.

Sulpicia (Roman poetess, aged 15)
Translated by John Heath Stubbs

SOFT CENTRE

I pull her hair
call out names,
join in all of
my mate's rough games.

I swagger past,
as she looks my way,
strong and silent,
nothing to say.

I mess about,
make out I'm tough,
but underneath
I'm soft enough.

And I'd really like
to hold her tight,
pause for a while
beneath streetlights,

buy her coffee,
talk until late,
kiss her goodnight,
tell her she's great.

But I'm meeting my mates
at the club tonight.
I couldn't do it,
it wouldn't be right.

So she smiles
and I scowl,
she speaks,
and I growl.

Brian Moses

BAKERY GIRL

I should have gone to find you
afterwards
to say:
sorry, I don't know me,
I wasn't listening when
my heart leapt
and I felt sick and
blind at the sight of you and
anxious
that my hair was
in place.

I should have responded with
happy, obvious flirtation
prettily, as you imagined
I would
positioning yourself so
to lean
casually against the price lists
Cornish pasties 79p.

But I forced my
face down
busily scribbling biro sums

on a paper bag which I
twirled twice and
gave to you
held out my hand and
turned away,
your voice drifting over me
somewhere
where I could or didn't
reach.

I should have met your eyes,
I should have reached over the
pie cabinet
when you leant towards me
and clasped
your face in my hands
and said
Yes
Yes
I am yours
scattering pastries.

Loveday Why

THE DAY BEFORE YESTERDAY

A horse doesn't know it has a forehead
until you smooth it with your hand.

Yesterday I closed my eyes at traffic lights
and remembered your arms.
Your hands stroked me a back,
your palms gave me shoulders,
your fingers left a new layer of skin.

And though our lips touched only twice
I swear you found a land within
where colour grows.

Chrissie Gittins

A SHY LAMENT

My love should be yours, but when I try
To speak, my lips are doors
Shut tight and I cannot ever tell you why
My love could be yours.

At school, I never learned the lover's laws,
The rules of what to do, when to say
I want to hold you, now my heart roars.

If I were thunder, dreaming of sky,
You, a bird that maybe soars
Then every kiss, that makes the wind sigh
My love, would be yours.

Polly Peters

GOT A DATE

I've got a date
with someone great.
And don't tell Mother
but if my brother
tries to spoil it,
I'll have to push him
Down the toilet.

Jill Townsend

LUV

I gorra luv meself,
that's wa' me grandad sez.
Gorra luv yerself, luv
coz nevva, no ways'll other folk
luv yer
if you don't luv yerself.

Gorra luv meself, he sez.
An' I do.

Joan Poulson

THE BENCH

I carved the letters deep with pride.
I scarred the rotting pine.
And now we lie here side by side
Your first name touching mine.

The rain may fade my traces and
The frost may blur your form.
But couples in embraces
Will keep our winter warm.

Rachel Rooney

LOVE: A LAD'S POEM

Ello darling, what's your name?
Not many of those to the pound, eh?
Ere love, I wanna show you something.
Sit on my lap babe, we'll chat about the first thing
  that comes up.
Ever know a real man?
Ere I am darling, your prayers are answered.
Asking for it she was.
Just don't understand women.

Bertel Martin

LONELY HEARTS

Superheroine:
Nine-feet high (with own cape) –
Wishes to meet
Superhero...

For outings to:
    burning buildings
    haunted castles
    snake pits
    and sinking ships.

Also: foreign travel – Mars,
Mercury, Jupiter, etc.

Must like:
    clubs (Karate)
    clothes (combat)
    bombs (unexploded)
    and car driving –
preferably off cliffs.

Also: pets – piranhas, sharks,
poisonous reptiles.

Please include photo.
    (No masks.)

Peter Dixon

FOR A LITTLE LOVE

For a little love, I would go to the end of the world
I would go with my head bare and feet unshod
I would go through ice, but in my soul forever May,
I would go through the storm, but still
hear the blackbird sing
I would go through the desert, and have pearls
of dew in my heart.
For a little love, I would go to the end of the world,
Like the one who sings at the door and begs.

(from Windows in a storm*)*
Jaroslav Vrchlicky
Translated by Vera Fusek Peters
and Andrew Peters

A HUG

Lie as close as nut to me
cupped darling in the acorn tree
Like goosegrass come cling close to me
Like grass your joys uncounted be
As pebble in stream be near to me
Like sea in shell your whisper be
Bird in nest be close but free
Bud to bloom on the rough rose tree
Lie as close as my heart to me.

Bruce Barr

SIX OF THE BEST

The six tastiest blokes
in our year have been devoured
by ravenous beauties.

The six most intelligent
have been ensnared without struggle
by the computer network.

The six with the best voices
have been conducted away to a choir
to perform an all-male sextet.

The six biggest posers
have been seduced by their own images
in a sweaty gymnasium.

The six most highly rated
have been captured by chess pieces
and reduced to stalemates.

Probably the best six-packs
have been consumed by their fear
of sober female reality.

The six wettest
have been stripped to their briefs
to practise breaststroke.

Those with six cylinders
have been navigated into the fast lane
by backseat lovers.

That only leaves the six
birdwatchers – and Milton Turton,
but I'm not that desperate!

Norman Silver

WHEN I SEE YOU

the fizz erupts again
in my flat cola.

When I see you
blossom invades
the winter trees

and the crowd
chants our names
endlessly, endlessly.

Someone writes them, linked,
high on a bridge
over the road home.

When I see you
the starlings in my garden
are parakeets and cockatiels.

Fred Sedgwick

CONNECTED SPECIES

He was well fit,
arse tight as a slipknot,
the two cheeks
a juicy pair of cherries.

He had a super-Stella six-pack,
hair so cool that penguins moved in
and a mind deep as the Titanic.

I dreamed of his tongue like the tide coming in;
the two of us a pair of electric eels
in ecstatic shock,
brought together by an
Act of Cod.

Year 9 group poem – Marches School, Shropshire

THE SONG OF WANDERING AENGUS

I went out to the hazel wood,
Because a fire was in my head,
And cut and peeled a hazel wand,
And hooked a berry to a thread;
And when white moths were on the wing,
And moth-like stars were flickering out,
I dropped the berry in a stream
And caught a little silver trout.

When I had laid it on the floor,
I went to blow the fire aflame,
But something rustled on the floor,
And someone called me by my name.
It had become a glimmering girl
With apple blossom in her hair
Who called me by my name and ran
And faded through the brightening air.

Though I am old with wandering
Through hollow lands and hilly lands,
I will find out where she has gone,
And kiss her lips and take her hands;
And walk among long dappled grass,
And pluck till time and times and are done
The silver apples of the moon,
The golden apples of the sun.

W B Yeats

LOVE'S PHILOSOPHY

The fountains mingle with the river
And the rivers with the Ocean,
The winds of Heaven mix for ever
With a sweet emotion;
Nothing in the world is single;
All things by a law divine
In one spirit meet and mingle.
Why not I with thine?

See the mountains kiss high Heaven,
And the waves clasp one another;
No sister-flower would be forgiven
If it disdained its brother;
And the sunlight clasps the Earth
And the moonbeams kiss the sea;
What is all this sweet work worth
If thou kiss not me?

Percy Bysshe Shelley

THE SCALE OF MY LOVE

On a scale of one to nine
I love you twenty-three
On a scale of grass to dandelion
I love you tree
On a scale of drip to puddle
I love you sea
My love for you is off the scales
You weigh the world to me

On a scale of nudge to bump
I love you ricochet
On a scale of sigh to smile
I love you hip hooray
On a scale of each second lived
I love you every day
On a scale of here to there
I love you all the way

Roger Stevens

45

TO HIS COY MISTRESS
– AN EXCERPT

Had we but world enough and time
This coyness lady were no crime.
We would sit down and think which way
To walk, and pass our long love's day...
But at my back I always hear
Time's wingèd chariot hurrying near:
And yonder all before us lie
Deserts of vast Eternity.
Thy beauty shall no more be found,
Nor, in thy marble vault, shall sound
My echoing song: then worms shall try
That long preserved virginity;
And your quaint honour turn to dust
And into ashes all my lust.
The grave's a fine and private place
But none I think do there embrace.
Now therefore, while the youthful hue

Sits on the skin like morning dew,
And while thy willing soul transpires
At every pore with instant fires,
Now let us sport us while we may,
And now, like amorous birds of prey,
Rather at once our time devour
Than languish in his slow-chapt power.
Let us roll all our strength, and all
Our sweetness, up into one ball:
And tear our pleasures with rough strife
Thorough the iron gates of life.
Thus, though we cannot make our sun
Stand still, yet we will make him run.

Andrew Marvell

MEET ME IN THE GREEN GLEN

Love meet me in the green glen
Beside the tall elm tree
Where the sweet briar smells so sweet agen
There come wi me
Meet me in the green glen

Meet me at the sunset
Down in the green glen
Where we've often met
By hawthorn tree and foxes den
Meet me in the green glen

Meet me by the sheep pen
Where briers smell at een
Meet me in the green glen
Where whitethorn shades are green
Meet me in the green glen

Meet me in the green glen
By sweet briar bushes there
Meet me by your own sen
Where the wild thyme blossoms fair
Meet me in the green glen

Meet me by the sweet briar
By the mole hill swelling there
When the west glows like a fire
God's crimson bed is there
Meet me in the green glen

John Clare

CARPE DIEM

O Mistress mine, where are you roaming?
O stay and hear! Your true-love's coming
   That can sing both high and low;
Trip no further, pretty sweeting,
Journeys end in lovers' meeting –
   Every wise man's son doth know.

What is love? 'tis not hereafter;
Present mirth hath present laughter;
   What's to come is still unsure:
In delay there lies no plenty –
Then come kiss me, Sweet-and-twenty,
   Youth's a stuff will not endure.

William Shakespeare

POEM WRITTEN ON A GARDEN WALL

A year ago I looked through this gate
and saw the face of a beautiful girl,
blushing peach-blossom pink.

I don't know where the girl is now,
or if she'll read this poem;
I can only see
the peach blossom laughing at me
in the warm spring breeze.

Cui Hu
Adapted by David Greygoose
from a translation by Shuhong Zheng

IF SHAKESPEARE HAD HAD A MOBILE

Shud i compare U 2 a summas day?
U R more lvly & more :-) babe:
Ruff winds shake the darlin buds of may
& summa is all 2 short a D8T:
Sumtime 2 hot the i ov heaven shines,
& often is his gold complexion dimm'd;
& every fair from fair sometime sez no
By chance or nature's course untrimm'd;
But yor mega summa won't fade
or lose possessn of that fair U R;
Or will death big it up that U hang in his pad,
When in eternal lines 2 time U grow:
So long as lads can breathe and i's can C,
So long lives this, and this gives life 2 U
txt bk lv will xxx

Steve Fisher

SHALL I COMPARE THEE TO A SUMMER'S DAY?

Shall I compare thee to a summer's day?
Thou art more lovely and more temperate;
Rough winds do shake the darling buds of May,
And summer's lease hath all too short a date:
Sometime too hot the eye of heaven shines,
And often is his gold complexion dimm'd;
And every fair from fair sometime declines,
By chance, or nature's changing course, untrimm'd;
But thy eternal summer shall not fade,
Nor lose possession of that fair thou ow'st;
Nor shall Death brag thou wander'st in his shade,
When in eternal lines to time thou grow'st;
So long as men can breathe, or eyes can see,
So long lives this, and this gives life to thee.

William Shakespeare

SMITH'S QUIFF

Stuck-up Smith coiffed his quiff,
Exercised his jaw,

Sensing scent, tense he went
At the sight he saw:

Gaggled girls, crimson curls,
Giggled at the door,

Grinned his way, Sharon, Kay.
Smith, he looked once more.

Lashes, black, flashed right back
Way across the floor.

Smith perceived, yes, believed
He they fluttered for.

Glossy lips, waggled hips,
Cheeks red-radish raw,

Legs from skirts, short as shirts
Beckoned: 'Je t'adore,'

So Smith thought. (He'd been caught!)
What could be in store...?

'Hiya Smith. Like your quiff,
's better than before',

Fingers twitched, eager, itched
Smith's quiff to explore –

Ruffled it, scruffled it.
Smith let out a roar!

Fled pell-mell, for his gel,
Down the corridor

In a tizz, bent on his
Image to restore.

Gina Douthwaite

THE PRETTIEST GIRL

My mates all stare as they see me pass
I'm dating the prettiest girl in class
and I note the way that their eyes are popping,
as she clings to my arms (she's taking me shopping)
while they'll be doing the same old things,
a game of footie beside the swings,
a spot of fishing down at the pool
then computer games and then, the fools
will be eating at joints where the food is fast.
Such childish things for me are past.
Yes, the gang will have to do without me
as I now have beautiful girls about me.
So I walk on by; I can't be stopping;
the prettiest girl is taking me shopping,
shopping in the Mall (I may have to pay)
shopping in the Mall (could be there all day)
shopping in the Mall (it's going to be boring)
shopping in the Mall (I'll soon be snoring)
and the gang all laugh as they see me pass,
stuck with the prettiest girl in class.

Marian Swinger

STONY

We found this secret beach
of sea-smooth stones last year;
what fun we had here!
We flung stones out to sea at first
over the running tide,
your lazy throws always the winners
no matter how hard I tried.
Then we bombed blobs of seaweed
with nearly fist-sized stones;
at hits or near misses
gave cheers or groans.
Then, leaning against two boulders,
arms round each other's shoulders,
we listened to shifting stones
in the tug and suck of the sea;
last year, you and me.

This year, remembering,
I walked the beach alone
and everything was cold
and grey as stone.

Eric Finney

AUTOGRAPH VERSE

If I were X and you were Y,
I'd stand by you and... multiply.
And once the two of us were paired,
Why, they would call us $(XY)^2$.

J Patrick Lewis

LOVE BUD

Do you carrot all for me?
My heart beets for you,
With your turnip nose
And your radish face.
You are a peach.
If we cantaloupe,
Lettuce marry;
Weed make a swell pear.

Anon

THE LOVER'S APPEAL

And wilt thou leave me thus?
　Say nay! Say nay! For shame!
　To save thee from the blame
　Of all my grief and grame.
And wilt though leave me thus?
　Say nay! Say nay!

　　　　And wilt though leave me thus,
　　　　　That hath loved thee so long
　　　　　In wealth and woe among?
　　　　　And is thy heart so strong
　　　　As for to leave me thus?
　　　　　Say nay! Say nay!

And wilt thou leave me thus,
　That hath given thee my heart
　Never for to depart
　Neither for pain nor smart?
And wilt though leave me thus?
　Say nay! Say nay!

　　　　And wilt thou leave me thus,
　　　　　And have no more pity
　　　　　Of him that loveth thee?
　　　　　Alas! Thy cruelty!
　　　　And wilt though leave me thus?
　　　　　Say nay! Say nay!

Sir Thomas Wyatt (1503-1542)

MY LUVE IS LIKE A RED, RED ROSE

Oh my luve is like a red, red rose
That's newly sprung in June:
Oh my luve is like the melodie
That's sweetly play'd in tune.

As fair art thou, my bonnie lass,
So deep in luve am I;
And I will luve thee still my dear,
Till a' the seas gang dry.

Till a' the seas gang dry, my dear
And the rocks melt wi' the sun;
And I will luve thee still, my dear
While the sands o' life shall run.

And fare thee weel, my only luve!
And fare thee weel a while!
And I will come again my luve,
Tho' it were ten thousand mile.

Robert Burns

MY LOVE IS LIKE A RED, RED ROSE – A PARODY

My love is like a red, red rose
That up the wall doth creep
One night you came and pulled it down
Threw it on the compost heap

My love is like a red, red rose
Entwined around a tree
But alas the rose grew suckers
And the biggest one was me

My love is like a red, red rose
That once you loved a lot
But now it's in a bed of weeds
with greenfly and black spot

My love is like a red, red rose
On a lovely summer's day
But winter's come and the garden's gone
It's now a motorway

Roger Stevens (after Robert Burns)

HATE

POEM

Get your tongue
out
of my mouth;
I'm kissing you
goodbye.

Ted Kooser

HATRED

Last week, I hated boys,
the way they growled,
the way they roamed like bears.
I loathed their clumsiness,
their clumpy feet,
their heavy, hostile stares.

Last week, I still despised
their greedy eyes,
their laughter harsh and low.
But one of them smiled down
at me! And now
my hatred melts like snow.

Clare Bevan

IT'S OVER, I KNOW

It's over, I know, and that means the end
of that world of our own we invented;
an end to coffee and holding hands
in that café we frequented;
an end to our secret hiding place
and the notes we left for each other
and an end to the different ways we found
to get rid of your little brother.
There'll be no more of those mobile phone chats
with you only ten yards away –
silly they seemed, but somehow
they made some things much easier to say.
There's a kind of aching emptiness left –
Sad that this should be how it ends.
I'm not sure how I'm going to cope
now we go back to just being friends.

Eric Finney

A REASONABLE AFFLICTION

On his deathbed poor Lubin lies:
    His spouse is in despair;
With frequent cries and mutual sighs,
    They both express their care.

'A different cause,' says Parson Sly,
    'The same effect may give:
Poor Lubin fears that he may die;
    His wife, that he may live.'

Mathew Prior (1664-1721)

I ASK FOR A DIVORCE

I ask for divorce.
You say it's the wrong time.
Irene just found the cat in the freezer.
Poor thing.
It will probably need some counselling,
Physio,
A spray of de-icer.
Life's too much of a rush right now.

I ask for a divorce.
You say things are too hectic right now.
The paper boy gave us the wrong tabloid.
Who's to say what's going on.
Don't ask me now.
I'm worrying about third-world debt
And Jeffrey Archer.
You'll consider it when you have more time.

I ask for a divorce.
You say things are getting worse by the day.
The stock market is falling.
Coal is running out. And if that's not enough
(you warn me in a whisper),
There may be Martians on Mars.
Life is getting on top of you.

I ask you for a divorce.
I can't look at you when I'm asking.
I'm not the villain here.
I don't know why I can see eight years in your eyes.
I don't know why I can see your hopes
Disappearing into the furrows of your brow.
I don't need an excuse when it's clear
That everything's changed.
I know you understand.

Kate Shipton (age 15)

GIVE ME BACK MY RAGS

Just come to my mind
and my thoughts will scratch out your face

Just come into my sight
and my eyes will start snarling at you

Just open your mouth
and my silence will smash your jaws

Just remind me of you
and my remembering will
paw up the ground under your feet

That's what it's come to between us

Vasko Popa
(Translated by Anne Pennington)

MARRIAGE GUIDANCE TUDOR STYLE...

No need to be queasy,
marital problems are easy:
you wed 'em and bed 'em,
then simply behead 'em

Matt Simpson

WHEN THE OLD CAT TREATS MILK WITH SCORN

When the old cat treats milk with scorn,
When the pigeon loathes its corn,
When the swan hates swimming, then
I'll come to court you, sulky Gwen.

Traditional Welsh poem
translated by Glyn Jones

SINCE YOU ARE YOUNG

(Apologies to W B Yeats)

Since you are young and brash, a handsome chap,
Who thinks he is the tops, take down this book,
And read about the boy who thought he shook
Up all the girls. It's such a load of crap.

How many think you look like some Greek god
And love your fine physique and tousled hair,
But when the lovelies take the questionnaire,
They all agree: You are a bleeding sod.

And bending down beside each doubtful miss,
You murmur, a little sadly, where Love went,
And now (insert the word for excrement),
You wonder when you might get your first kiss.

J Patrick Lewis

THE WIFE'S LAMENT

May my man's mind be made miserable,
And tortured, the twist of his heart.
May he wear a smile, but his guts be in grief
In the whole wide world,
May he only love himself.
And make him a reject, a refugee
far from friends in foreign lands.
Stick him under stones,
my bad-mouthed man,
storm-soaked in a shoddy shack.
My old beloved, be full of fear;
remember where you used to live.
Sorrow is the prize for love that ends in pain.

Anglo-Saxon poem
(translated by Andrew Fusek Peters)

THE LONG WAITING

This place that I most hate
this space, these cobweb hours
this chair, this plastic jug
that bloody vase, I loathe.
The smell of flowers makes me retch
the cellophane uncurls inside the bin.
Above the shelf, a box of rubber gloves
and sterile wipes I want to tear.
I hate the way your slippers lie,
they bear the indentation of your weight,
the steady press of feet now still.
I hate the squeak of rubber soles
outside this room, that step in other's lives.
Your hands are moths,
I hate to see the bruising of your veins
and hanging up, a coat for which you have
   no need.

Your eyes are closing doors
I hate the autumn folding of your breath.
You lie, a curling leaf,
Your weight and hair now shorn.
And I detest that you're too young
And so am I, for this:
As you fed me, now I feed you. It's wrong.

I hate the empty spaces in our house
where you once were.
I hate the photos in their frames.
I hate that you won't see the adult I'll become
I hate that you are weak and I am strong.

But later, when I whisper
'See ya later, alligator'
I shall hold my breath
and will it to be true.

Polly Peters

I WISH

I wish I was curvy, I wish I was pretty
instead of being straight all the way down and zitty.
I wish I had hair like the adverts on telly,
I wish I had long legs like my best friend Kelly,
I wish that my brace didn't glint when I chatter,
and I'm really too skinny. I wish I was fatter.
I wish that I didn't look just like my aunt,
and wish I could have a body transplant
for I always expected, on entering my teens
to look like the models do in magazines.
I wish, as I pass that the boys would all whistle
and later, compose me romantic epistles.
I wish I was famous, an idol, a star,
but a girl with my looks doesn't get very far
and I wish above all, that my dad wouldn't say,
'And how is my beautiful girl?' every day.

Marian Swinger

I AM SO A CROSS STIC

Desperately
Unhappy
My
Pillow's
Extremely
Damp!

Steve Fisher

MIXED EMOTIONS

My first shows in helping and not in hurting,
My first is in heartless – not caring or kind,
My next in supporting and not subverting,
My second – in anger and malice you'll find,
My third is in valuing never in scorn,
My third starts the trouble I spread everywhere,
My fourth is in friends – where I'm normally born,
My fourth dwells in misery, torment and fear.

Philip Waddell

Hate

I took what I hated
to a corner of the school yard.
I battered it, I bust its nose,
I shoved it through the railings.

That didn't help. I took it
to the road and pushed it – oops –
underneath a bus, a steamroller, a tank.
It was no use. I dropped it
off a railway bridge, a cliff,
an aeroplane. I crunched it
with a 200-tonne weight. I stuck it
with a million pins. I tore it apart.
I played football with the bits.

That didn't help. It was no use.
It kept looking at me, winking disgustingly.
I was shaking all over. I woke up.
I was banging my own head on the wall.

Dave Calder

CHOICES

She doesn't choose where she lives
or the school, the uniform
but she can choose small things:

which bus to miss, how to hang about
for the moment to slip down corridors and stairs

to try and become invisible, not there,
to dodge sneers and shoves, taunts, threats,
the torment of the toilets, the playground.

She doesn't tell her parents, she chooses
not to tell her teachers. Why?

Come on, we all know why. Think of when
you were afraid and powerless. Think
what you chose. She chooses silence

and the cuts and pills, later,
she will choose them as well.

Dave Calder

THE BULLY

The bully's thoughts
are like a grey-grim tower block,
instead of trees, graffiti grows
and every smile is under lock
and key.

The bully's anger must be made a crime,
loitering with fists,
disturbing the face,
joy-hiding,
killing time.

The bully's eyes are tarmac-dark,
crushing all who dare to grass,
his driven mind an empty space
in a concrete-cold car park.

The bully's fingers
make a fist of twisted spoons
stirring up hate
to cook us in,
his heart, the emptiest of balloons,
full of hot air,
unable to care.
Has anyone got a pin?

Andrew Fusek Peters

CIRCUS OF FRIENDS

From the first day of term, we were
Like a magic circle it seemed.
We were big, we were top,
We were cream of the crop,
Meant to be friends to the end. We were
Unbreakable, unshakeable, un-sepa-rateable,
'Til those Strongmen muscled on in
And divided our act with their power to pull,
Tearing friendship limb from limb.

Knife-like words were expertly thrown,
But always hit too close for comfort.
Never piercing the skin or breaking the bone
The damage went deeper within.

I became acrobatic
And bent myself double,
Jumping through hoops just to please.
I braved it alone
On the high-wire of friendship,
But mixed loyalties always weigh heavy.

Then while juggling it all,
Without the aid of a net,
They cavorted around me like clowns.
And tripping each other they trapped me
   with ease
And brought our great act to its knees.

Just at the time we needed each other,
Our friendship was falling apart.
And as I frantically tried
To break the fall,

Like lions,
They went straight for the juggler.

Damian Harvey

I TRULY LOVED MY SWEETHEART

I truly loved my sweetheart
For more than one whole year,
My heart thinking he held me
To be his only dear,
And I his happy sweetheart
With a garden flower's appeal –
I was just bread and butter
Sliced ready for his meal.

Traditional Welsh poem, translated by Glyn Jones

ANGER LAY BY ME ALL NIGHT LONG

Anger lay by me all night long,
  His breath was hot upon my brow,
He told me of my burning wrong,
  All night he talked and would not go.

He stood by me all through the day,
  Struck from my hand the book, the pen;
He said: 'Hear first what I've to say,
  And sing, if you've heart to, then.'

And can I cast him from my couch?
  And can I lock him from my room?
Ah no, his honest words are such
  That he's my true-lord, and my doom.

Elizabeth Daryush

STICKS AND STONED

On the last day of term
The bastard got so drunk, he passed out in
   assembly.
A river of spew splashed from his mouth
As the head carried on
About the term's achievements.

The day before,
I lost it.
That is, I lost whatever says you should or
   shouldn't do.
Found his locker, desk, papers, books
And screamed
As I tore and crumpled his work and words
   To pieces.

And for once, the teasers, the taunters
   backed off
'Easy now!' As if I were a wild one
As if I, surrounded by the golden glow of hate,
   Made of my anger a river
   That fell from my fists.

   After,
   He looked at me different...
   Still with a sneer,
   But uncertain at my edges.

   My friends, it was mental and magnificent!
   I recommend it.

   Andrew Fusek Peters

85

COUNTING DAYS

It's been six days, I've kept my silence well.
I give a yes or no, a stunted phrase.
My mother sighs, I don't think she can tell
the anger's gone. I'm simply counting days.

I didn't wipe the crumbs up, words were said
then later screamed across the bedroom door.
What started off as fussing over bread
becomes a full blown mother-daughter war.

The bread's gone stale. My mother cannot wait.
She asks why I'm choosing not to speak.
I hesitate and shrug. I calculate
That I can hold my silence for a week.

Rachel Rooney

SAD CHANGE

(a Chaucerian roundel)

My mother and my father row
each day. They've rowed for years.
It often ends in angry tears.

'What magic curse changed them, and how?'
I ask each day amid my fears.
My mother and my father row.

They loved each other once – but now?
They're like two cars with grinding gears.
My heart is bruised by what it hears.
My mother and father row.

John Kitching

THE QUESTION

What twist of hate
And sleight of hand?
Shall we ever
Understand
How a mind
Can grow so wild?
How a body
Snatch a child?
Does Murder have
A mother dear?
What the birthplace
Of such fear?
Where did Motive
Go to school?
What family taught him
To be cruel?
Was Love buried
In a grave?
Oh this world,
So new, so brave
Where all our dreams
Now decompose,
Sing the lily and the rose
In the forest
Of the night
Hold our dear ones,
Dear ones, tight.

Andrew Fusek Peters

SPIKESFILOSOFY

doan
doan wannago
doan wannago
toscool
cosscools
uncool

doan
doanwannalern
doanwannalern
nuffin

doan
doan wannreed
buksan
doan wannado
pee ee

doan
doan wannabe
toldattodo

doan
doan wannalern
istoryan
alldatstuf
dayteechus

wannabe
wotiwannabe

wannabefree
datsformee

Tony Langham

THEY HUNTED THE GYPSIES

They hunted the Gypsies
in Europe's great towns:
they hunted and murdered
to bring them all down.

**Hunted and murdered
to bring them all down.**

They marked them with numbers
tattooed on their wrist:
they beat them and bruised them
with jackboot and fist.

**Beat them and bruised them
with jackboot and fist.**

They dressed them in tatters,
scalps pitted with cuts:
starved them and threw them
in crowded damp huts.

**Starved them and threw them
in crowded damp huts.**

They gassed them in chambers
where no light could shine:
they took out the bodies
and laid them in line.

    Took out the bodies
    and laid them in line.

They burned them in ovens
with the scapegoats and Jews:
but who'll tell the world
of this sinister news.

    Who'll tell the world
    of this sinister news.

They hound today's travellers
from roadside and town:
but no one will force them
to bend or kneel down.

    No, no one can force them
    to bend or kneel down.

John Rice

BRUISES HEAL

Names, cold shoulders,
Silence in the canteen
Her words are scalpels,
Cutting self-esteem.

Stuck up little cow!
Thinks she's really it!
Laughter slices, she prescribes
A sharp, unfunny wit.

Ridiculed for standing out,
My marks are much too high
And so she drip-feeds saline hate,
Injecting with a lie.

She's bright, she'll find
The weakest spot to pierce
  and prod and poke.
She uses stealth, and poisoned words
And wears them like a cloak.

It seems I am her favourite game
And I'm the one who loses,
If she'd done this with her fists,
At least there would be bruises.

Polly Peters

DON'T DO

You want me to smile
but that's just futile
Cos it's not my style.
It says in my file
That I don't
        do
          happy

                    Now, I'm hard to rile,
                    no venom, no bile.
                    I'm not volatile,
                    in fact I'm docile
                    but I don't
                            do
                              don't
                              do
                                happy.

So it's not worth your while
to tell me to smile.
Accept my denial
and end this vile trial
cos I don't
      do
       don't
      do
       don't
      do
       happy.

Nick Toczek

MY
BEST
MATE

RECIPE TO MAKE A GOOD FRIEND

Shoulders (broad)
A level head
Eyes (insensitive to red)
Skin (immune to slights not due)
A neck (that will stick out for you)
   Loads of guts (but lack of bile)
Funny bones
A ready smile
Goalie's hands (to save the day)
Feet (but note – not made of clay)

For someone good
   those parts now blend
But adding these will
make a friend...

A heart (concerned about your fate)
And kindred soul (to ani-mate)

Philip Waddell

PERFECT BLEND

She's a:
Sadness safe-cracker
A down-in-the-dumps hijacker
A deepest-secret keeper
A talk-for-hours non-sleeper
An automatic-advice dispenser
A future candidate for Mensa
An Olympic-qualifying talker
A hold-head-high-whatever walker
A listener to all my woes
The fear-of-God to all my foes

A promise fulfiller
Gossip killer
Dance all-nighter
Tiredness fighter
Solid shoulder
For things I've told her

She's my:
Round the bend, got to spend
Quick to lend, own trend
Perfect blend
Best friend!
(what would I do without her?)

Polly Peters

MY BEST MATE

He's a fart composer
Dull-lesson dozer
Beyond belief
Boredom thief
Hang around benches
Chatting up wenches
Make me ecstatic
Footie fanatic
More than enough
When times are rough
Up all night,
Guess he's all right
Swearing,
Daring
Even caring
One to rate
Hard to hate
My best mate.

Andrew Fusek Peters

SONNET 138
BY WILLIAM SHAKESPEARE

When my love swears that she is made of truth,
I do believe her though I know she lies,
That she might think me some untutored youth,
Unlearned in the world's false subtleties.
Thus vainly thinking that she thinks me young,
Although she knows my days are past the best,
Simply I credit her false-speaking tongue;
On both sides thus is simple truth suppressed.
But wherefore says she not she is unjust?
And wherefore say not I that I am old?
O love's best habit is in seeming trust,
And age in love loves not to have years told.
Therefore I lie with her, and she with me,
And in our faults by lies we flattered be.

ME AND MY MATE
- PARODY

When my mate said, 'Your secret's safe, it's cool',
She grinned and winked. Me, I was terrified.
I knew that it was going round the school
And yet, it wasn't simply that she lied.
She lives for gossip, tasty little bites
Which bring an evil glimmer to her eye –
This guy, that toilet, or a pair of tights.
She's hooked. And, if I'm honest, so am I.
I ought to know by now, so if I'm wise
I shouldn't share the really secret stuff
But I can't help myself. Surprise, surprise,
The world knows who I fancy. Well, that's tough.
She's still my mate. Really, she's not that bad.
Mind you, last night she went out with this lad…

Paul Francis

OF PERFECT FRIENDSHIP

True friendship unfeigned
Doth rest unrestraigned
No terror can tame it:
Nor gaining, nor losing,
Nor gallant gay glosing,
Can ever reclaim it.
In pain, and in pleasure,
The most truest treasure
That may be desired,
Is loyal love deemed
Of wisdom esteemed
And chiefly required.

Anon (1579)

THEY MIGHT
NOT NEED ME

They might not need me – yet they might –
I'll let my heart be just in sight –
A smile so small as mine might be
Precisely their necessity.

Emily Dickinson

LUV MY BRUV

My brother is the James Bond of Year 10.
His lunchtime-corridor-lounging look
Leaves girls shaken and stirred.
I'm not jealous,
Though he's got four years on me, armpit hair
And a voice so craggy it's criminal.

When Wayne Knowles mimicked my squeak
In the boys' loos,
His laugh was cut short
By a well executed kick in the goolies.
As Wayne whined and clutched his privates,
My brother smirked
'You're havin' a ball now, sonny!'

'I feel like a, cigarette,' I say.
'You don't look like one!' he laughs
as he puffs out these perfect little frisbees,
And gives me tips about French kissing.
When we played Spin The Bottle,
I got to snog his girlfriend,
On the bench, at the park,
In a lake of neon light
Our tongues whirled like bumper cars:
Thanks to my brother,
the James Bond of Bottle,
I was in O O Heaven!

Andrew Fusek Peters

DAMIAN

1. Tumour

The last time we met
was the first time
I'd heard the word.
The last time we met,
you came into school
a horseshoe scar inverted
So the luck runs out
in the stubble of your head.
The last time we met,
you saw me as a stranger,
remembering nothing of the past,
the last time we met
in a playground
of averted eyes and rumour.

2. Blocked Out

The invented card games
and secret codes,
the fight when I thought
you'd broken my nose,
the magic tricks
that never worked
and the mind reading
that did
forgotten the penknife
pricking our thumbs
as we called each other brother,
forgotten how, aged twelve
I heard you were dead.

Kevin McCann

BODY PIERCING

My mate Stacey has got five earrings in each ear
She's got a bar through her eyebrow
a stud in her nose
her tongue pierced
and her belly button.
Unfortunately last week, during games
she met with a nasty accident.
She got hit by a javelin!
Ironic that, don't you think?

Steve Fisher

BLOOD TIES

Bloody hell, bloody cow
Not another bloody row
Bloody called me bloody fat
Won't bloody get away with that
Bloody fist now watch it curl
Bloody fly at bloody girl
Bloody scream, bloody thud
Bloody nose with bloody blood
Bloody give me bloody eye
Bloody painful, bloody cry
Bloody finished, bloody done
Not a lot of bloody fun
Bloody dabbing bloody eyes
Bloody won't apologise
Bloody silence, bloody stare
Darlin', I don't bloody care
Bloody filled with bloody hate
Bloody miss my bloody mate

Andrew Fusek Peters

THERE WERE
THESE TWO GIRLS

there were these two girls
strutting down the street
whistling
loud enough to crack the windows

they were whistling
at the moon
but the moon just winked
as it hid behind a cloud

they were whistling
at the lampposts
but the lampposts just blinked
as they leaned together
like drunks

they were whistling
at the boys
who slinked off round the corner
like shamefaced puppies
with their tails between their legs

they were whistling
at the world
then they stood there listening
to see
if the world would whistle back

Dave Ward

GIRLS AWAKE, ASLEEP

Young girls up all hours
devouring time-is-money on the phone:
conspiracies of mirth,
sharp analyses of friends' defects,
confession, slander, speculation
– all the little mundane bravenesses
that press the boundaries
of what can be thought, felt and talked about.
Their clear-voiced punctuation rings
up stairwells, to where parents toss
and groan, a sense of their own tolerance
some consolation for short nights, long bills.

Young girls in bed all hours
fathom sleep oceans,
drink oblivion with their deep breaths,
suck it like milk.
Curled round their own warmth,
they fat-cat on the cream of sleep
lapping dreams.
For this, they will resist all calling.
Surfing the crests of feather billows
they ride some sleek dream animal,
pulling the silk strands of his name,
urging him on.

Carole Satyamurti

ROUNDABOUTS

Hey, you heard the latest on Sharon, right?
You know, sister of Stu
Mouthy bird, oh what's her name?
Was once best mates with you.

Yeah, Sharon right, with the mousy hair
Knocked round with Michael Dene
Well, Debs saw her necking that Kevin Thing
In the youth club down Kensal Green.

No, not *that* Kevin, the other one
Used to be mates with Dan
Who had the hots for Suzie Potts
Before he dumped her for Ann.

No, *Suzie's* not going with Spanner
Listen! you stupid or what?
She's into a heavy scene with Spike
Who used to knock round with Dot.

You know, *Dot* with the bleached-out roots
Who left that Dave for Spike
And *she* only stuck with him so long
Because of his motorbike.

Yeah, *that* Dave, had a Mohican
Once went out with Rose
Till she saw him one night in the park with
    that girl
And belted him one up the nose.

That girl? You know who I mean
Spiteful and highly strung
Talks about people behind their backs
Her name's on the tip of my tongue.

Oh Come on, you know who I mean
Dumpy and really plain
Always slagging people off
You know er... Oh What's her Name?

Spotty and always rabbiting on
No better than she ought to be
Wait a minute, it's all coming back
This girl...
I think it was me.

Gareth Owen

PROVERBIAL FRIENDSHIP

'he ain't heavy – he's my brother...'

A stone from a friend
becomes an apple.
For love of Allah,
Hallaj on the cross
could not feel the stones
hurled at his body,
but cried out in pain
when a friend struck him
with a soft flower.

Join hearts together
but keep tents apart
for fear such closeness
leads to enmity.
If someone hates you,
consider what good
turn did you do them.
The worst enemy
is your dearest friend.

Friendship does not mean
you never quarrel.
It knows the joy of
making up again.
When we cut the cord
of friendship and tie
the ends together,
the cord is shorter
and we grow closer.

Debjani Chatterjee

Note: Mansur Al Hallaj was a tenth-century
Sufi mystic who was crucified by order of the
caliph Al Muqtadir

SOME FRIENDS

Some friends
Are like magnets
They stick close when you face
But as soon as your back's turned, they
Repel

Damian Harvey

IF I WERE A WITCH

If I were a witch I would think of a curse
may she grow pimply, toothless or worse.
If I ruled the world as a ruthless dictator,
she'd be my first victim. I really hate her.
If I was head teacher, I would expel her.
I hate her, I hate her; will nobody tell her?
I shall loathe and despise her for time without end,
for she, who pretended to be my best friend,
she, who dumped me for that fat old cow,
certainly isn't my best friend now.
Let her creep, let her crawl, let her beg,
let her plead;
she's a best friend I for one, do not need.

That's what I wrote in my diary last night,
but we made up today, so, well, hey, that's all right.

Marian Swinger

THIS IS WHAT YOU DO

This is what you do:
you hook your little fingers together
you shake them up and down
and say this rhyme

make friends make friends
never never break friends

This is what you do:
you hold your door for your friend in the school
  toilets
you give her half of your packed lunch KitKat
you plait each other's plaits

make friends make friends
never never break friends

This is what you do:
you snarl and squabble
you cry and quarrel
you don't speak for days

until Miss Pike says
If you want to have a friend
you have to be a friend

and at your side
you hear your friend whisper
if you want to have a Mars Bar
you have to be a Mars Bar

and you die laughing
and the quarrel's nothing
until the next time.

This is what you do:
you go to playschool
you go to big school
you go to secondary

you hook your little fingers together
you shake them up and down
and say this rhyme

and it stays true
time after time
for all the breaking.

Helen Dunmore

index by title

Anger Lay By Me All Night Long	Elizabeth Daryrush	83
Asking Out	Jim Hatfield	16
Asnogstick	Steve Fisher	12
Autograph Verse	J Patrick Lewis	58
Bakery Girl	Loveday Why	28
Bean Picking	Brian Moses	22
Bench, The	Rachel Rooney	33
Blood Ties	Andrew Fusek Peters	109
Body Piercing	Steve Fisher	108
Boy With Green Hair	Pauline Fisk	8
Bruises Heal	Polly Peters	92
Bully, The	Andrew Fusek Peters	78
Carpe Diem	William Shakespeare	50
Choices	Dave Calder	77
Circus of Friends	Damian Harvey	80
Connected Species	Marches School, Shropshire	41
Counting Days	Rachel Rooney	86
Damian	Kevin McCann	106
Day Before Yesterday, The	Chrissie Gittins	30
Don't Do	Nick Toczek	94
First Kiss	Eric Finney	20
Fone Fantasy	Alison Chisholm	24
For A Little Love	Jaroslav Vrchlicky	36
(translated by Vera Fusek Peters and Andrew Fusek Peters)		
Girls Awake, Asleep	Carole Satyamurti	112
Give Me Back My Rags	Vasko Popa	68
Got A Date	Jill Townsend	32
Hate	Dave Calder	76
Hatred	Clare Bevan	63
His First Love	Brian Patten	6
Hug, A	Bruce Barr	37
I Am So A Cross Stic	Steve Fisher	75
I Ask For A Divorce	Kate Shipton	66
I Truly Loved My Sweetheart	Anon	82
(translated by Glyn Jones)		
I Wish	Marian Swinger	74
If I Were A Witch	Marian Swinger	119
If Shakespeare Had Had A Mobile	Steve Fisher	52
It's Out At Last	Sulpicia	25
(translated by John Heath Stubbs)		

It's Over, I Know	Eric Finney	64
Lonely Hearts	Peter Dixon	35
Long Waiting, The	Polly Peters	72
Love Bud	Anon	58
Love Kept Secret – an excerpt	Dafydd ap Gwilym	13
	(a version by Andrew Fusek Peters)	
Love Letters	Clare Bevan	14
Love: A Lad's Poem	Bertel Martin	34
Lover's Appeal, The	Sir Thomas Wyatt	59
Love's Philosophy	Percy Bysshe Shelley	44
Luv	Joan Poulson	32
Luv My Bruv	Andrew Fusek Peters	104
Marriange Guidance Tudor Style	Matt Simpson	69
Me And My Mate – a parody	Paul Francis	01
Meet Me In The Green Glen	John Clare	48
Mixed Emotions	Philip Waddell	75
My Best Mate	Andrew Fusek Peters	9
My Love Is Like A Red, Red Rose – a parody	Roger Stevens	61
	(after Robert Burns)	
My Luve is Like A Red, Red Rose	Robert Burns	60
My Mate Fancies You	Polly Peters	10
Of Perfect Friendship	Anon	102
Overheard Behind The Lockers	Matt Simpson	18
Perfect Blend	Polly Peters	98
Poem	Ted Kooser	63
Poem Written On A Garden Wall	Cui Hu	51
(adapted by David Greygoose – from a translation by Shuhong Zheng)		
Prettiest Girl, The	Marian Swinger	56
Proverbial Friendship	Debjani Chatterjee	116
Question, The	Andrew Fusek Peters	88
Reasonable Affliction, A	Mathew Prior	65
Recipe To Make A Good Friend	Philip Waddell	97
Roundabouts	Gareth Owen	114
Sad Change	John Kitching	87
Scale Of My Love, The	Roger Stevens	45
Shall I Compare Thee To A Summer's Day		
	William Shakespeare	53
Shy Lament, A	Polly Peters	31
Since You Are Young	J Patrick Lewis	70
Six Of The Best	Norman Silver	38
Smith's Quiff	Gina Douthwaite	54
Soft Centre	Brian Moses	26
Some Friends	Damian Harvey	118

Song of Wandering Aengus, The	W B Yeats	42
Sonnet 138	William Shakespeare	100
Spikesfilosofy	Tony Langham	89
Sticks And Stoned	Andrew Fusek Peters	84
Stony	Eric Finney	57
There Were These Two Girls	Dave Ward	110
They Hunted The Gypsies	John Rice	90
They Might Not Need Me	Emily Dickinson	103
This Is What You Do	Helen Dunmore	120
To His Coy Mistress – an excerpt	Andrew Marvell	46
When I See You	Fred Sedgwick	40
When The Old Cat Treats Milk With Scorn	Anon	69
	(translated by Glyn Jones)	
Wife's Lament, The	Anon	71
	(translated by Andrew Fusek Peters)	

index by author

Anon	Love Bud	58
	Of Perfect Friendship	102
Anon	When The Old Cat Treats Milk With Scorn	69
(translated by Glyn Jones)	I Truly Loved My Sweetheart	82
Anon (translated by Andrew Fusek Peters)	Life's Lament, The	71
Bruce Barr	Hug, A	37
Clare Bevan	Love Letters	14
	Hatred	63
Robert Burns	My Luve is Like A Red, Red Rose	60
Dave Calder	Choices	77
	Hate	76
Debjani Chatterjee	Proverbial Friendship	116
Alison Chisholm	Fone Fantasy	24
John Clare	Meet Me In The Green Glen	48
Elizabeth Daryrush	Anger Lay By Me All Night Long	83
Emily Dickinson	They Might Not Need Me	103
Peter Dixon	Lonely Hearts	35
Gina Douthwaite	Smith's Quiff	54
Helen Dunmore	This Is What You Do	120
Eric Finney	First Kiss	20
	Stony	57
	It's Over, I Know	64
Steve Fisher	Asnogstick	12
	If Shakespeare Had Had A Mobile	52
	I Am So A Cross Stic	75
	Body Piercing	108

Pauline Fisk	Boy With Green Hair	8
Paul Francis	Me And My Mate – a parody	101
Chrissie Gittins	Day Before Yesterday, The	30
Dafydd ap Gwilym	Love Kept Secret – an excerpt	13
(a version by Andrew Fusek Peters)		
Damian Harvey	Circus of Friends	80
	Some Friends	118
Jim Hatfield	Asking Out	16
Cui Hu (adapted by David Greygoose – from a translation by		
Shuhong Zheng)	Poem Written On A Garden Wall	51
John Kitching	Sad Change	87
Ted Kooser	Poem	63
Tony Langham	Spikesfilosofy	89
J Patrick Lewis	Autograph Verse	58
	Since You Are Young	70
Marches School, Shropshire	Connected Species	41
Bertel Martin	Love: A Lad's Poem	34
Andrew Marvell	To His Coy Mistress – an excerpt	46
Kevin McCann	Damian	106
Brian Moses	Bean Picking	22
	Soft Centre	26
Gareth Owen	Roundabouts	114
Brian Patten	His First Love	6
Andrew Fusek Peters	Bully, The	78
	Sticks And Stoned	84
	Question, The	88
	My Best Mate	99
	Luv My Bruv	104
	Blood Ties	109
Polly Peters	My Mate Fancies You	10
	Shy Lament, A	31
	Long Waiting, The	72
	Bruises Heal	92
	Perfect Blend	98
Vasko Popa	Give Me Back My Rags	68
Joan Poulson	Luv	32
Mathew Prior	Reasonable Affliction, A	65
John Rice	They Hunted The Gypsies	90
Rachel Rooney	Bench, The	33
	Counting Days	86
Carole Satyamurti	Girls Awake, Asleep	112
Fred Sedgwick	When I See You	40
William Shakespeare	Carpe Diem	50
	Shall I Compare Thee To A Summer's Day	53
	Sonnet 100,	138
Percy Bysshe Shelley	Love's Philosophy	44

Kate Shipton	I Ask For A Divorce	66
Norman Silver	Six Of The Best	38
Matt Simpson	Overheard Behind The Lockers	18
	Marriange Guidance Tudor Style	69
Roger Stevens	Scale Of My Love, The	45
Roger Stevens (after Robert Burns)	My Love Is Like A Red, Red Red Rose – a parody	61
Sulpicia (translated by John Heath Stubbs)	It's Out At Last	25
Marian Swinger	Prettiest Girl, The	56
	I Wish	74
	If I Were A Witch	119
Nick Toczek	Don't Do	94
Jill Townsend	Got A Date	32
Jaroslav Vrchlicky (translated by Vera Fusek Peters and Andrew Fusek Peters)	For A Little Love	36
Philip Waddell	Mixed Emotions	75
	Recipe To Make A Good Friend	97
Dave Ward	There Were These Two Girls	110
Loveyday Why	Bakery Girl	28
Sir Thomas Wyatt	Lover's Appeal, The	59
W B Yeats	Song Of Wandering Aengus, The	42

acknowledgements

The compilers and publisher gratefully acknowledge permission to reproduce the following material:

Anvil Press Poetry for *Give Me Back My Rags* taken from 'Vasko Popa: Collected Poems' translated by Anne Pennington, revised and expanded by Francis R Jones. Published by Anvil Press Poetry in 1997;
Eirlys Barr for Bruce Barr's *A Hug* © The Estate of Bruce Barr;
Clare Bevan for *Hatred* and *Love Letters*;
Bloodaxe Books for Carole Satyamurti's *Girls Awake, Asleep*, in 'Selected Poems' (Bloodaxe Books, 2000);
Dave Calder for *Hate* and *Choices*;
Carcanet Press for Elizabeth Daryrush's A*nger Lay by me All Night Long*, in 'Selected Poems';
Laura Cecil Literary Agency for Norman Silver's *Six of the Best* © 1993 Norman Silver 'The Comic Shop' published by Faber and Faber Ltd;
Debjani Chatterjee for *Proverbial Friendship*;
Alison Chisholm for *Fone Fantasy*;
Combrogos Literary Agency for Glyn Jones' *When the Old Cat...* and *I Truly Loved My...*, in English translation;
Peter Dixon for *Lonely Hearts*, from 'Penguin in the Fridge' by Peter Dixon (Macmillan 2001);
Gina Douthwaite for *Smith's Quiff*, in 'Our Side of the Playground' (The Bodley Head, 1991);

Eric Finney for *It's Over I Know*, First Kiss and Stony;

Steve Fisher for *I Am So A Cross Stick, Body Piercing, If Shakespeare Had Had a Mobile* and *Asnogstick*;

Pauline Fisk for *Boy with Green Hair*;

Paul Francis for *Me and My Mate*;

Andrew Fusek Peters for *The Wife's Lament, For a Little Love, The Bully* from 'The Weather's Getting Verse' (Sherbourne, 1996), *Sticks and Stoned, The Question, My Best Mate, Luv My Bruv, Blood Ties* and *Love Kept Secret*;

Chrissie Gittins for *The Day Before Yesterday*;

Jim Hatfield for *Asking Out*;

Damian Harvey for *Some Friends* and *Circus of Friends*;

Hearing Eye Press for *It's Out at Last*, reprinted by permission of the publishers, from 'The Poems of Sulpicia' (Hearing Eye 2000) translated by John Heath-Stubbs, ISBN 870841751;

John Kitching for *Sad Change*;

Tony Langham for *Spikesfilosophy*;

J. Patrick Lewis for *Since You Are Young* and *Autograph*;

Bertel Martin for *Love: A Lad's Poem*;

Kevin McCann for *Damian*;

Brian Moses for *Soft Centre*, first published in 'Knock Down Ginger and Other Poems' by Brian Moses (Cambridge University Press, 1994) © Brian Moses, and Bean Picking © Brian Moses 2003;

Gareth Owen for *Roundabouts*;

Polly Peters for *Bruises Heal* from 'Poems with Attitude' (Hodder Wayland, 2001), *The Long Waiting, My Mate Fancies You, A Shy Lament* and *Pefect Blend*;

Joan Poulson for *Luv*;

John Rice for *They Hunted the Gypsies*;

Rogers, Coleridge & White Ltd for *His First Love*, copyright © Brian Patten, 2003. Reproduced by permission of the author c/o Rogers, Coleridge & White Ltd; 20 Powis Mews, London W11 1JN;

Rachel Rooney for *Counting Days* and *The Bench*;

Fred Sedgwick for *When I See You*;

Kate Shipton for *I Ask for a Divorce*;

Matt Simpson for *Marriage Guidance Tudor Style* and *Overheard Behind the Lockers*;

Roger Stevens for *The Scale of My Love* and *My Love is Like a Red Red Rose;*

Marian Swinger for *If I Were a Witch, I Wish* and *The Prettiest Girl*;

Nick Toczek for *Don't Do*;

Jill Townsend for *Got a Date*;

Philip Wadell for *Recipe to Make a Good Friend* and *Mixed Emotions*;

Dave Ward for *There Were These Two Girls* and *Poem Written on a Garden Wall*;

AP Watt Ltd for WB Yeat's *The Song of Wandering Aengus*, reproduced by permission of A.P Watt Ltd on behalf of Michael B Yeats; and for Helen Dunmore's *This is What You Do* © Helen Dunmore;

Loveday Why for *Bakery Girl*.

Biography

Andrew Fusek Peters and Polly Peters are highly esteemed authors and editors. Between them, they have produced over 35 critically acclaimed titles – storybooks, picture books, graphic novels, verse novels, anthologies and poetry collections. Their best-selling teenage collections – *Poems with Attitude* and *Poems With Attitude, Uncensored* – were both Guardian Education book of the week. Look out for their teenage verse novel – *Crash* – and Andrew's graphic novels – *Ed and the Witchblood* and *Ed and the River of the Damned*. Andrew is currently writing a teenage novel entitled *The Vinegar Coffin*, which is based on Andrew's family's experiences during World War Two. You can find more information about their books on www.tallpoet.com

'A very effective mix of old and new ... The modern and classic often juxtaposed in striking ways ... Highly recommended.'

School Librarian